T Is for Tiger

ROCKRIDGE
PRESS

For general information on our other products and services or to obtain technical support, please contact our Customer Care Department within the United States at (866) 744-2665, or outside the United States at (510) 253-0500.

Rockridge Press publishes its books in a variety of electronic and print formats. Some content that appears in print may not be available in electronic books, and vice versa.

Cover and interior illustrations by Laura Watkins
Interior and Cover design by Creative Giant Inc
Editor: Lia Brown

ISBN: Print 978-1-64152-480-3 | eBook 978-1-64152-481-0

R1

A is for albatross and alligator!

Alligators like to eat fruit as well as meat and fish.

Bears will walk for miles to scratch their backs on their favorite tree!

B is for bear,
butterfly,
and beaver.

C is for cardinal,
chipmunk,
and cat.

Cats love naps.
They sleep 16 hours a day!

D is for dog
and dolphin.

E is for eagle
and elephant.

Elephants are the largest land animals on earth.

F is for frog, fox, and flamingo.

A flamingo's feathers get their color from the food they eat.

G is for giraffe, gazelle, and gorilla.

Mountain gorillas share human emotions. They laugh when tickled and cry when hurt, just like you.

H is for heron, horse, and honeybee.

Great blue herons are about three feet tall but weigh only about six pounds.

I is for iguana.

Iguanas can break off their tails to escape danger. Sometimes their tails grow back!

J is for jaguar.

The spots on a jaguar's fur are called rosettes because they look like roses!

is for kookaburra, kangaroo, and koala.

Kangaroos and Koalas are
both a type of mammal
called a marsupial.

Lovebirds mate for life.

L
is for lovebirds
and lions.

M is for moose
and mouse.

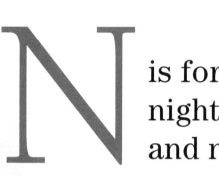

N is for newt,
nightcrawler,
and nightingale.

The nightingale's song is
so beautiful, it has become
a symbol of love.

O is for osprey, orca, and otter.

Mother otters and their pups hold
on to each other while sleeping.

P is for python, porcupine, and parrot.

A python tastes the air with its tongue to smell if food is nearby.

Q

is for quokka.

The shape of a quokka's mouth looks
like a smile, which may be why they are
called the world's happiest animal!

R is for rabbit.

S is for shark,
seal, and starfish.

Baby sharks and baby
seals are both called pups!

T is for tiger,
turtle, and
tortoise.

The tiger is the
biggest species of
the cat family!

U
is for urial.

Urials move their ears to show
whether they are happy or sad.

V

is for Vicuña.

Vicuña live high in the mountains.
Their fur keeps them warm at night.

Beluga whales are able
to swim backwards!

W

is for walrus,
whale, and wolf.

X is for xantus.

Y is for yak.

Yaks use their horns to break through the
snow to uncover plants they like to eat.

Z is for zebra.

Every zebra has a unique pattern
of stripes. That may be how they
recognize each other!

Each animal representing a letter of the
alphabet might be found living near one another
in a specific part of the world. Some animals
featured are just one kind from many different
"families" within their species.

Turn the page to learn more about
the animals in the book.

Where in the world?

A

North America
Albatross
Alligator – American

B

North America
Bear – Black Bear
Beaver – North American
Butterfly – Eastern
Tiger Swallowtail

C

North America
Cardinal – Northern
Cat – Domestic
Chipmunk

D

North America
Dog – Domestic
Dolphin – Bottlenose

E

Africa
Eagle – African fish
Elephant – African

F

Asia
Flamingo – Greater
Fox – Bengal
Frog – South Indian

G

Africa
Gazelle – Thomson's
Giraffe – West African
Gorilla – Mountain

H

North America
Heron – Great Blue
Honeybee
Horse – North American
(though not native)

I

Central America
Iguana – Green

J

Central and South America
Jaguar

K

Australia
Kangaroo – Red
Koala
Kookaburra – Laughing

L

Africa
Lion
Lovebird – Fischer's

M
North America
Moose
Mouse – Deer

N
Western Europe
Newt – Alpine
Nightcrawler
Nightingale

O
North America
Orca
Osprey
Otter – Sea

P
Asia
Parrot – Alexandrine
Porcupine – Himalayan
Python – Burmese

Q
Australia
Quokka (pronounced Kwa-ka)

R
Western Europe
Rabbit

S
Ocean
Seal – Brown Fur
Shark – Great White
Starfish – Red

T
Asia
Tiger – South China
Tortoise – Indian Star
Turtle – Indian Black

U
Central Asia
Urial (pronounced You-ree-al)

V
South America
Vicuña (pronounced Vy-coo-nya)

W
The Arctic
Walrus
Whale – Beluga
Wolf – Arctic

X
Baja California, Mexico
Xantus (pronounced Zan-tus)

Y
Asia
Yak

Z
Africa
Zebra – Plains

Where in the world?

The Arctic

North America

Central America

South America

LAURA WATKINS

Laura has been passionate about stories and drawing since she was a child. Pads of paper were not enough, so reels of wallpaper ended up suiting her better. She has worked on international children's books, cards, painted murals, and art galleries. Laura lives in an old rickety house in London. When not painting, she is busy building wonky furniture and renovating her houseboat.

For Stark, Palla, Jank, Frabs, & KT — Laura

CPSIA information can be obtained
at www.ICGtesting.com
Printed in the USA
JSHW021206290720
6976JS00008B/111